MW01205955

FROM	TO

WWW.TWISTEDCITY.IT

Made in the USA
Coppell, TX
20 May 2024

32579721R00085